Published By Adam Gilbin

@ Paul Platt

Meditation: Finding Peace in Everyday Life the

Only Introduction You'll Ever Need

All Right RESERVED

ISBN 978-87-94477-63-5

TABLE OF CONTENTS

chapter 1	1
Exploring Types Of Meditation	1
Chapter 2	5
Mindfulness Meditation Overview	5
Chapter 3	11
The Journey Begins	11
Exploring The Power Within	11
Chapter 4	17
Understanding Meditation	17
Chapter 5	26
Meditation And Making Money	26
Chapter 6	36
Choosing Your Meditation Space	36
Chapter 7	39
Chapter 8	45
Fundamentals Of Mindfulness Meditation	45
Chapter 9	49

Mindfulness Meditation 49

Chapter 10 59

What Is Mindful Living? 59

Chapter 11 64

The Origins And Evolution Of Meditation 64

Chapter 12 69

Establishing Your Mindfulness Practice 69

Chapter 13 75

Embracing Mindfulness And Meditation 75

Chapter 14 82

A Simplified Guide For Beginners 82

Chapter 15 86

Getting Started With Mindfulness Meditation 86

Chapter 16 89

Preparing For Meditation 89

Chapter 17 92

Chapter 1
Exploring Types of Meditation

Guided Meditation

Guided meditation, also known as guided imagery or visualization, transcends mere stillness. It's a journey orchestrated by a guide or teacher, leading you through mental landscapes of calmness. This practice engages multiple senses—invoking the fragrance of serene places, the visuals of peaceful scenes, the sounds that soothe, and the textures that ground. Guided meditation is an artful immersion into the discovery of calming images, offering a guided escape from the hustle of everyday life.

Mindfulness Meditation

At the heart of mindfulness meditation lies an invitation to embrace the present moment with heightened awareness. This practice revolves around expanding conscious awareness, focusing on the nuances of the "now." The breath becomes a guide, a steady anchor in the ebb and flow of experiences. Overall, mindfulness meditation brings awareness to thoughts and emotions and promotes a connection with the present moment.

Yoga

Yoga, a fusion of postures and controlled breathing, transcends the physical body. It beckons you to a union of body and mind, promoting flexibility and calmness. Each pose is a deliberate step towards mindfulness, requiring balance and concentration. Yoga serves as a moving meditation, urging you to be fully present as you gracefully traverse through a sequence of postures.

Qi Gong

Rooted in traditional Chinese medicine, Qi Gong is a holistic practice harmonizing meditation, relaxation, physical movement, and breath control. This dynamic fusion aims to restore and maintain the delicate balance of energy within. Qi Gong's rhythmic movements, accompanied by intentional breath work, create a symphony that attunes the body's energy, fostering a profound sense of equilibrium.

Tai Chi

Tai Chi, a slow and graceful manifestation of Chinese martial arts, seamlessly connects meditation with movement. Performing a series of postures and movements with deliberate precision, Tai Chi is a dance of balance and poise. Deep breathing accompanies each motion, cultivating a serene state of mindfulness. It's a martial art transformed into a moving meditation, a dance of tranquility in slow motion.

These are just a few types of meditation practices that I have chosen to share. As a beginner, the path unfolds most gracefully when guided, the purpose of this beginner's book. In the subsequent chapters, we will delve into the art of being guided through the meditation process. But before we venture further, let's explore the rich array of benefits that meditation gracefully bestows upon those who embark on this transformative journey.

CHAPTER 2

Mindfulness Meditation Overview

Finding a respite from the turmoil becomes critical amid the rush and bustle of modern life when every moment appears to demand our attention. This is where mindfulness meditation comes into play, a practice that has grown in popularity in recent years due to its capacity to foster a sense of presence and awareness. Mindfulness meditation is fundamentally about being focused in the present moment, devoid of distractions from the past or fears from the future. We will go into the essence of mindfulness meditation, its benefits, and practical strategies for incorporating it into our lives in this investigation.

Recognizing Mindfulness Meditation
Mindfulness meditation has its roots in ancient contemplative traditions, dating back to Buddhist

practices. Its secular application, on the other hand, has made it accessible to individuals from all walks of life, regardless of religious or cultural roots.

Mindfulness is defined as giving one's attention to the current moment without judgment. It is not a matter of emptying the mind, but of noticing ideas and sensations as they emerge.

One of the most important aspects of mindfulness is growing awareness via techniques that focus attention on the present moment. This frequently entails focusing on the breath, physiological sensations, or a specific point of attention. The idea is not to remove thoughts, but to watch them detachedly, allowing them to pass like clouds.

According to research on mindfulness meditation, persistent practice can lead to brain changes linked with greater attention, emotional control, and even structural changes in areas involved with self-awareness and empathy. Individuals who practice mindfulness may discover a stronger ability to respond carefully to life's obstacles rather than reacting impulsively.

The Advantages Of Mindfulness Meditation
Mindfulness meditation has been shown to improve physical, mental, and emotional well-being. One of its key benefits is stress reduction. Individuals can stop the cycle of stress and create a mental space for clarity and peace by cultivating a nonjudgmental awareness of thoughts and emotions.

Mindfulness meditation has also been linked to increased attention and cognitive capacities. Regular practice improves focus and attention, helping people to be more present and engaged in their everyday tasks. This improved awareness can lead to more informed decisions and higher productivity.

Mindfulness can help people build a better emotional relationship with their thoughts and feelings. It enables emotional recognition without becoming overwhelmed by them. This emotional resilience is especially useful in dealing with anxiety and depression since it gives a tool for navigating the mind's intricacies.

Mindfulness meditation has also been related to improved physical health. According to research, it can help with blood pressure control, immunological function, and sleep.

Mindfulness techniques highlight the mind-body link, emphasizing the comprehensive nature of its effects and fostering general well-being.

How To Begin Mindfulness Meditation

Beginning a mindfulness meditation journey does not need a complex setup or substantial training. Here are some practical steps to get you going:

Find a peaceful Place: Select a peaceful location where you will not be disturbed. This might be a room nook or a tranquil outside situation.

Sit or lie down in a posture that is comfortable for you. The goal is to be relaxed while remaining vigilant. Sit on a cushion or chair with your back straight and your hands on your lap.

Close your eyes and concentrate your attention on your breath. Take note of how each inhale and exhale feels. If your thoughts begin to wander, gently bring them back to the breath.

Body Scan: Another option is to do a body scan. Begin with your toes and work your way up through each portion of your body. Observe any tension or feelings without passing judgment.

Guided Meditations: Use guided meditations, which are available through numerous applications or online platforms. These frequently include a structured meditation session given by an experienced meditation teacher.

Begin with small sessions, perhaps 5-10 minutes, and gradually increase the length as you grow more comfortable with the practice.

Remember that the purpose is to observe the present moment with acceptance and non-judgment, not to reach a certain condition.

Chapter 3

The Journey Begins

Exploring the Power Within

In the heart of every person lies an extraordinary potential waiting to be discovered. It's a power that transcends the ordinary, a force that can shape destinies and overcome even the most daunting challenges. Welcome to the beginning of your transformative journey where you embark on the exploration of the incredible power within you.

The Call of Self-Discovery

Imagine standing on the edge of a vast, uncharted wilderness. You sense the thrill of the unknown, the tingling anticipation of what lies beyond the horizon. Your heart beats with a mixture of excitement and trepidation. This wilderness represents your inner self—a terrain rich with possibilities, talents, and dreams waiting to be realized.

But how often do we venture into this wilderness? How often do we heed the call of self- discovery? In the hustle and bustle of everyday life, it's easy to ignore the whispers of our innermost desires, drowned out by the cacophony of responsibilities and expectations. Yet, deep within, there's a longing for something more—for a life infused with purpose, confidence, and fulfillment.

Unraveling the Layers

To embark on this journey, we must first understand the layers that shroud our true selves. These layers are woven from experiences, beliefs, and societal influences, creating a tapestry that often obscures our authentic essence. It's like peeling an onion; with each layer removed, we inch closer to the core of our being.

One significant layer is self-awareness the foundation upon which personal transformation is built. Self-awareness is the mirror that reflects our thoughts, emotions, strengths, and weaknesses. It's about recognizing our patterns of behavior, understanding our triggers, and acknowledging our deepest desires.

In this chapter, we will delve into the heart of self-awareness, unveiling the power of knowing oneself intimately.

The Power of Self-Awareness

Self-awareness is not merely a theoretical concept; it's a practical tool that empowers us in every aspect of life. When we are self-aware, we make conscious choices aligned with our values and aspirations. We become attuned to our intuition, allowing it to guide us on our journey. Moreover, self-awareness strengthens our emotional intelligence, enabling us to navigate complex social situations with grace and empathy.

Consider the story of Maya, a young woman who felt trapped in a monotonous job, longing for a career that ignited her passion. Through self-awareness, she identified her interests, values, and strengths. Acknowledging her love for creativity and communication, she transitioned into a field that aligned with her authentic self. Today, Maya thrives as a successful graphic designer, her work infused with the vitality of her true passion.

Your Personal Exploration

As you read these words, I invite you to pause for a moment of reflection. Consider your own layers the experiences that have shaped you, the beliefs that have influenced your decisions, and the dreams that have yet to be realized. Imagine peeling away those layers, one by one, until you stand face-to-face with your authentic self.

In the chapters that follow, we will embark on this exploration together. We will unravel the complexities of your identity, celebrate your strengths, and embrace your vulnerabilities. Through engaging exercises, inspiring stories, and insightful reflections, you will uncover the power within you—a power that holds the key to your personal transformation.

Are you ready to embark on this adventure? Are you prepared to delve deep into the wilderness of your soul, discovering the treasures that lie within? If so, turn the page and let the journey begin. Let us explore the uncharted territories of your inner self and unlock the extraordinary power that resides within you. Your adventure starts now.

Chapter 4

Understanding Meditation

Contemplation, frequently covered in misguided judgments and persona, is a training that rises above social limits, time, and convictions. At its center, contemplation is a flexible instrument that offers a significant method for interfacing with oneself and the world. In this section, we'll disentangle the quintessence of contemplation, dispersing fantasies and diving into its importance for teens and youthful grown-ups in the present clamoring world.

The Essence of Meditation

At its heart, meditation is tied in with developing an elevated condition of mindfulness and presence. As opposed to mainstream thinking, it's not exclusively about exhausting the psyche of contemplations but rather about noticing considerations without connection or judgment. It's the specialty of being completely present at the time, recognizing the sensations inside the body, the considerations crossing the thoughts, and the feelings emerging without getting caught in them.

Debunking Myths Surrounding Meditation

One of the most generally perceived off-track decisions is that reflection is solely for those searching for significant brightening or individuals segregated from everyday presence. Genuinely, consideration is an open practice for anyone searching for clearness, up close and personal harmony, and flexibility, especially inside the exceptional presence of adolescents and young adults.in

Benefits of Meditation for Teenagers and Young Adults

The high school years are a period of fast change, self-disclosure, and profound choppiness. Reflection gives a tool stash to explore these difficulties. The research proposes that standard contemplation practice can lessen pressure, further develop concentration and focus, upgrade profound guidelines, and encourage a more noteworthy feeling of prosperity.

For teens adjusting scholarly tensions, extracurricular exercises, and social elements, contemplation offers a safe haven — a space to re-energize, gain clearness, and foster a more profound comprehension of oneself amid the chaos.

Types of Meditation Practices

Reflection is definitely not a one-size-fits-all training. There are different techniques taking care of assorted inclinations and requirements.

Care reflection, where consideration is centered around the current second, breath, or substantial sensations, fills in as a phenomenal beginning stage. Directed representation permits the brain to investigate distinctive mental symbolism, developing smoothness and innovativeness. Development-based reflections, for example, yoga or strolling contemplation take care of people looking for a more unique methodology.

Beginning Your Reflection Process

Leaving on a reflection venture doesn't need excellent arrangements. It's essentially as straightforward as tracking down a peaceful space, expecting an agreeable stance — whether sitting or resting — and focusing on the breath or a picked point of convergence. Novices could find it accommodating, to begin with, short meetings, slowly expanding length as solace and knowledge of the training develop.

Developing an Outlook for Reflection

Persistence and consistency are key in the act of reflection. It's essential to move toward contemplation with a receptive outlook, understanding that considerations will normally emerge during the training. Instead of feeling deterred, treating these minutes with thoughtfulness and delicately directing the concentration back to the picked point of consideration is fundamental.

Integrating Reflection into Day to day existence

Contemplation isn't bound to formal practice meetings; it can penetrate day-to-day existence. Straightforward care practices like careful eating or pausing for a minute to zero in on breathing during changes between exercises can imbue snapshots of quiet and presence into the most active of days.

Benefits of meditation :

Meditation is a powerful practice that has been shown to have a wide range of benefits for both physical and mental health. Some of the most well-documented benefits of meditation include:
Reduced stress and anxiety: Meditation can help to reduce the levels of stress hormones in the body, leading to a decrease in feelings of stress, anxiety, and tension.

person meditating in a peaceful environment
Improved sleep: Meditation can help to promote better sleep by calming the mind and body. It can also help to reduce insomnia and other sleep problems.

person sleeping peacefully in a bed
Increased focus and concentration: Meditation can help to train the mind to stay focused and present, leading to improved focus and concentration in daily life.

person studying with a focused look

Reduced blood pressure: Meditation has been shown to lower blood pressure, which can help to reduce the risk of heart disease and stroke.

healthy heart

Improved pain management: Meditation can help to reduce the perception of pain, and it can also help to improve mood and well-being in people who su er from chronic pain.

person meditating with a pain relief balm

Increased self-awareness: Meditation can help to increase self-awareness, leading to a better understanding of one's own thoughts, feelings, and behaviors.

person looking at their reflection in a mirror

Reduced reactivity to emotional triggers: Meditation can help to reduce reactivity to emotional triggers, leading to a more calm and composed response to di cult situations.

person meditating with a calm face

Improved cognitive function: Meditation has been shown to improve cognitive function, including memory, attention, and problem-solving skills.

person meditating with a brain puzzle

Increased creativity: Meditation can also help to boost creativity by clearing the mind and promoting new ideas.

person meditating with a paint brush and a canvas

Improved relationships: Meditation can help to improve relationships by promoting greater understanding, compassion, and empathy.

couple meditating together

In addition to these specific benefits, meditation has also been shown to have a number of other positive effects on health and well-being, including:

Reduced risk of depression

Improved immune system function

Reduced inflammation

Increased longevity

Meditation is a safe and effective practice that can be enjoyed by people of all ages and backgrounds. There are many different types of meditation, so it is important to find one that works best for you. If you are new to meditation, there are many resources available to help you get started, including books, websites, and apps.

Please note that meditation is not a substitute for professional medical treatment. If you are struggling with a mental health condition, please seek professional help

Chapter 5

Meditation and Making Money

The connection between meditation and making money is not complicated. It depends on how meditation can affect a person's mindset, choices, and overall happiness.

Meditating can help improve your mental focus and clarity. It can also enhance your ability to make decisions, including financial ones. By learning to focus your attention and block out distractions, you can make more thoughtful and informed financial decisions. Meditation can greatly increase your clarity and focus, benefiting decision-making in all areas of life, including finances. By practising deep concentration and staying present in the moment, you can make more logical and well-informed financial management decisions. This improved mental clarity can also help you better understand complex financial issues, assess risks, and plan for the long term.

Also, meditation helps people stay calm when the market goes up and down or when they're dealing with money-related stress. It makes them emotionally stronger and less likely to act impulsively, which helps them avoid making hasty financial choices that could be bad.

Ultimately, meditation helps you think more clearly and stay focused. This can lead to making better financial plans, which can help you create wealth and be financially secure.

Reducing Stress: Meditation is a great way to reduce stress. Money worries can cause a lot of stress. When you meditate regularly, it helps improve your mental and emotional well-being by reducing stress. This makes it easier for you to think clearly about your financial goals and plans.

Financial stress is something many people deal with, but meditation can help relieve some of that burden. By practising meditation regularly, you can significantly lower your stress levels and feel calmer. This will help you approach financial decisions and problems with more clarity and strength because you'll have a better emotional balance.

Meditation can help you handle your money worries and anxiety by reducing stress. It not only improves your overall mental and emotional well-being, but also helps you make better financial plans with a clear mind. By avoiding the negative effects of stress, you can assess your financial goals, make thoughtful decisions, and navigate economic challenges more effectively. Meditation helps you feel more relaxed and financially stable.

Meditation helps you get more stuff done. Studies show that it makes you more productive and efficient. This can lead to getting paid more and moving up in your career. Meditating regularly helps you focus, manage your time better, and be more effective overall. It's been proven by lots of research. Being more productive at work can bring you all kinds of good things, like making more money and getting promoted. Meditation can help people become more aware and think more clearly. This can be really helpful for getting things done faster and making smart decisions. When people meditate, they also get better at handling stress and taking care of their responsibilities, which can make them do better at work. Plus, being more productive can help them move up in their career and get recognised for their hard work. So, in the end, meditation is a great way to improve professionally and be happier with your job.

Having a positive mindset is really important. When you meditate, it helps you feel hopeful and upbeat. Being positive can bring in opportunities and help you make money. It also helps you overcome obstacles and disappointments, which are common on the path to financial success. Meditation can have a big impact on your financial journey by helping you have a happy mindset. When you're positive, you attract opportunities and open doors to making money. When you stay positive, you see obstacles as chances to learn and grow. This is important for achieving financial success because it helps you overcome challenges with confidence and determination.

Having a positive attitude can also make you more creative and better at solving problems, which can be really helpful when it comes to finding new and creative ways to handle your finances. When you approach money decisions with a positive mindset, you're more likely to make smart investments and take reasonable risks. Meditation can help you stay positive about making money, which can give you the confidence to overcome challenges and reach your financial goals.

Meditation helps you control your emotions and stay strong. It's important to be emotionally stable when dealing with money because the markets can be unpredictable. Meditation can help investors avoid making impulsive decisions based on greed or fear. Emotional control is crucial in finance, and meditation is a key way to develop it. Investing and managing wealth can be stressful and make you feel anxious or greedy. Meditation gives you the tools to stay calm and make smart financial choices.

While meditation won't guarantee wealth, it can be a helpful addition for those aiming to succeed financially. It provides a strong foundation for mental and emotional well-being, enhancing their capacity to make smart financial choices, handle challenges, and take advantage of opportunities.

How can I visualize wealth generation?

Visualization for becoming wealthy: -

Take a nice deep breath and then just close your eyes. Picture yourself on a really nice day in a calm garden. Feel the warm sun on your skin; it's like a cosy hug, kind of like having enough money to feel secure.

Make sure you look for the beautiful colours and lush scenery as you explore this garden. Each flower represents an idea or opportunity to make money. You can feel the softness of the petals, just like how creative thoughts come to you easily, by touching them.

Now take a seat on a cozy bench. Clarify in your mind what your financial objectives are. Watch the balance in your bank account increase over time. Imagine the satisfaction of having a surplus of money and no debt. Your mental sharpness and composure serve as a compass to direct you towards wealth.

Just sit back and enjoy the calming sound of the birds chirping. It's a reminder that you don't have to worry about money. Picture all your financial problems fading away like dew in the morning sun. You're in control here, so there's no need to stress.

Picture this: there's a laptop sitting on a desk in a beautiful landscape. When you open it up, you become super-efficient and get a lot done. Your hard work pays off, and your investments start growing like blooming flowers. Every move you make helps you achieve financial success.

Imagine yourself right now shining with positivity. Your positive outlook draws possibilities, and your optimism functions as a magnet for success. Knowing that every obstacle is a step closer to your financial objectives, you accept each one with a smile.

Take a moment to think about this. You now know a lot about yourself. You know what you value, how much risk you're comfortable with, and what your long-term financial goals are. When it comes to investing, you make choices based on this self-awareness, so that they align with what you want to achieve financially.

You find a cool fountain while walking in the garden after waking up. The water is full of clever ideas for making money. When you take a drink, you start thinking of creative business ideas and investment plans.

Finally, imagine inviting your friends and coworkers to come join you in this garden. Your relationships get stronger because of your positive attitude and financial success. Just like the flowers around you, partnerships and collaborations start to grow, opening up new opportunities for making money.

Slowly open your eyes now, and remember that you always have the potential for prosperity and well-being within you. Throughout your day, keep this vision in mind and let it guide you towards achieving financial success.

Chapter 6

Choosing Your Meditation Space

When it comes to mindfulness meditation, choosing the right space can make all the difference. Here are some things to consider when selecting your meditation space:

Space and Stability

It's important to choose a space that is quiet and free from distractions. Find a place where you won't be disturbed during your meditation practice. If possible, choose a space that is stable and secure, such as a room with a door you can close. This will help you feel safe and protected during your meditation practice.

Comfort and Support

It's important to choose a comfortable place to sit or lie down during your meditation practice. This will help you stay focused and relaxed. You may want to use a cushion or chair to support your back and help you maintain good posture.

Surroundings and Environment

Choose a space with a calming environment that supports your practice. You may want to decorate your meditation space with items that bring you peace and tranquillity, such as candles, incense, or plants. Make sure the room is well-ventilated and at a comfortable temperature.

Personal Preferences

Ultimately, the best meditation space is one that feels comfortable and supportive to you. Experiment with different spaces and find what works best for you. Some people prefer to meditate outside in nature, while others prefer a quiet room indoors. Listen to your body and mind, and choose a space that feels right for you. By taking the time to choose the right meditation space, you can create a supportive environment that helps you stay focused and relaxed during your mindfulness meditation practice.

CHAPTER 7

Introduction to Pranic Healing Meditation

Through the profound yogic technique of Pranic Healing Meditation, one can access the ancient wisdom of harnessing prana, the life force energy. This can open doors to potential for abundance, spiritual growth, and holistic well-being. This chapter explores the fundamental elements of Pranic Healing Meditation, illuminating its essence, tracing its historical origins, and emphasizing its distinctive characteristics that distinguish it from other forms of meditation.

Understanding Pranic Healing Meditation's Fundamentals:

Fundamentally, prana and meditation are two powerful components that are combined to create Pranic Healing Meditation. Prana, which is sometimes described as the life-giving energy, is said to permeate all living things, energizing and supporting life itself. In contrast, the practice of meditation involves intentionally focusing attention and achieving a deep level of awareness. As the name implies, prana is channeled and manipulated through meditation techniques in prana healing meditation, which promotes emotional balance, physical healing, and spiritual elevation.

How to Use Pranic Healing Meditation is based on the belief that many physical, emotional, and mental illnesses can result from imbalances or obstructions in the prana flow. People can enhance their health and vitality by intentionally directing and accessing this energy stream, which can activate the body's natural healing processes. Additionally, this method works on mental unrest and promotes a profound sense of inner serenity in addition to the physical.

Examining Pranic Healing's Historical Foundations and Origins:

The roots of prana healing can be found in esoteric knowledge systems and ancient yogic traditions that have been passed down through the ages. References to prana and energy manipulation can be found in many different cultures throughout the world, including Chinese Qi Gong, Japanese Reiki, and Indian Ayurveda, however the exact roots may be lost to the mists of time.

The ancient Indian yogic traditions are intimately connected to the origins of Pranic Healing Meditation. For a very long time, yogis and spiritual masters have understood the importance of prana and how it contributes to reaching greater consciousness and overall wellbeing. This wisdom has been honed and organized over the millennia into a methodical technique, which has culminated in the contemporary discipline of Pranic Healing Meditation.

How Pranic Healing Meditation Differs from Other Meditation Methods:

Although many people practice meditation, Pranic Healing Meditation stands out due to its emphasis on manipulating prana for transformation and healing. Pranic Healing Meditation actively involves the practitioner in harnessing and directing prana to address particular physical, emotional, or spiritual needs, in contrast to standard mindfulness meditation, which stresses monitoring thoughts and sensations without attachment.

Additionally, Pranic Healing Meditation differs from other meditation techniques such as Transcendental Meditation (TM) and Zen meditation, which focus mostly on reaching a state of expanded awareness and mental calm. While each of these methods has advantages of its own, Pranic Healing Meditation adds a new level of energetic engagement that enables people to take an active role in their own healing process.

Moreover, the underlying idea of Pranic Healing Meditation is that prana may be methodically moved and manipulated by employing particular procedures. This practical method makes working with energy accessible and empowering for anyone, including those who are not familiar with energy work or meditation. It provides practitioners with a concrete foundation.

To sum up, Chapter 1 offers a thorough overview of Pranic Healing Meditation, revealing its core as a combination of prana and meditation, delving into its historical origins in ancient yogic traditions, and emphasizing its distinctive methodology in setting itself apart from other meditation styles. As this book progresses, readers will learn more about the subtleties of Pranic Healing Meditation and discover how it can be used to advance spiritual enlightenment, prosperity, and good health.

Chapter 8

Fundamentals of Mindfulness Meditation

In this chapter, we will delve deep into the practice of mindfulness meditation. This is a form of meditation that has gained prominence due to its profound benefits for the mind, body, and spirit. Mindfulness meditation, also known as mindfulness, is a technique that allows us to be completely present in the moment, without judgment or distraction. It's like taking a deep dive into the pool of your own consciousness.

The Essence of Mindfulness Meditation

Mindfulness meditation has ancient roots, originating from Buddhist practices, but it is a skill that anyone can develop, regardless of their cultural or religious background. The essence of mindfulness meditation is to pay full attention to the present moment. This means being fully aware of what is happening within and around you, without judging or getting carried away by thoughts and emotions.

To begin, find a quiet place where you can sit comfortably. Close your eyes and start to breathe deeply. Notice the sensation of your breath as it enters and exits. If your mind begins to wander, don't worry; this is normal. Just redirect your attention back to your breath.

The Power of Observation

Observation is the key to mindfulness meditation. As you practice, you will begin to notice thoughts, emotions, and sensations that previously went unnoticed. You become an observer of your own mind, watching the constant flow of thoughts and feelings. This can be revealing, as we often are not aware of the patterns that govern our lives.

Imagine that your mind is a clear, open sky, and your thoughts are clouds passing by. Instead of clinging to these clouds or trying to push them away, you simply observe them. This attitude of acceptance and non-judgment is essential in mindfulness meditation.

The Benefits of Mindfulness Meditation

Regular practice of mindfulness meditation has numerous benefits. It helps reduce stress, anxiety, and depression. It also improves concentration and mental clarity, allowing you to make more conscious and precise decisions. Furthermore, mindfulness strengthens emotional resilience, making it easier to cope with life's challenges.

When you are present in the moment, you experience a deep sense of peace and contentment. This doesn't mean you won't face challenges, but that you will have the ability to confront them with calm and balance.

Becoming a Skillful Practitioner

Mindfulness meditation is not something you master overnight. It is a journey of self-discovery and self-transformation. As you practice regularly, you will begin to notice the benefits accumulating in your life. However, it's important to be patient with yourself and not expect immediate results. Moreover, remember that mindfulness meditation is not limited to formal meditation sessions. It can be incorporated into your daily life, whether by practicing mindfulness while eating, walking, driving, or engaging in any other activity. The more you practice, the deeper and more enriching your experience becomes. Mindfulness meditation is a fascinating journey into yourself, an exploration of your own mind, and a powerful tool to enhance your quality of life. As we progress through this book, you will learn more about advanced mindfulness meditation techniques and how to apply them in your daily life. Enjoy the journey of self-discovery and the awakening of mindfulness.

Chapter 9

Mindfulness Meditation

What Is Mindfulness Meditation?

Mindfulness meditation is a transformative practice that invites you to be fully present in the moment, observing your thoughts, feelings, and sensations without judgment. This technique has its roots in ancient Buddhist traditions and has gained widespread popularity for its effectiveness in reducing stress, enhancing self-awareness, and promoting emotional well-being.

The Essence of Mindfulness

At its core, mindfulness is about cultivating awareness. It involves paying deliberate and non-judgmental attention to your experiences, whether they're happening internally (your thoughts and emotions) or externally (your surroundings and interactions).

The Observer Within

Mindfulness encourages you to become the observer of your own mind. It's like stepping back and watching your thoughts and emotions from a distance, without getting entangled in them. This separation allows you to gain insights into your thought patterns and emotional responses.

A Path to Greater Clarity

By practicing mindfulness, you can develop a clearer understanding of your mind and emotions. This clarity can help you respond to life's challenges with greater wisdom and composure.

A Life-Changing Skill

Mindfulness is not just a meditation technique; it's a skill that you can integrate into your daily life. With mindfulness, you can navigate the complexities of life with more intention, resilience, and joy.

Practicing Mindfulness in Daily Life

The true power of mindfulness lies in its integration into your daily routine. You don't need to be in a quiet room to practice mindfulness; you can infuse it into every moment of your life.

Mindful Eating

Start with something as simple as mindful eating. Pay close attention to the flavors, textures, and smells of your food. Slow down and savor each bite, allowing yourself to fully enjoy the experience.

Mindful Walking

While walking, focus on the sensation of your feet touching the ground. Be aware of the movements of your body as you walk. Mindful walking can turn a mundane activity into a deeply meditative experience.

Mindful Communication

Practice mindful communication by actively listening to others. Be fully present in the conversation, giving the other person your undivided attention. This can lead to more meaningful and harmonious relationships.

Mindful Stress Management

During moments of stress, pause and take a few mindful breaths. Observe your thoughts and emotions without reacting impulsively. This can help you respond to stressors with greater calm and clarity.

Mindful Breathing Meditation

Mindful breathing meditation is a fundamental practice in mindfulness. It serves as a cornerstone for cultivating present-moment awareness.

Find a Quiet Space

Begin by finding a quiet space where you won't be interrupted. Sit comfortably on a cushion, chair, or the floor. Close your eyes if you prefer.

Awareness of Breath

Direct your attention to your breath. Notice the sensation of your breath as it enters and leaves your nostrils or the rise and fall of your chest or abdomen.

Let Go of Distractions

As you breathe, you may notice thoughts, feelings, or sensations arise. Instead of getting caught up in them, acknowledge their presence and gently bring your focus back to your breath.

Non-Judgmental Observation

Observe your breath without judgment. It's not about achieving a particular state but about being with your breath, just as it is.

Mindful Body Scan Meditation

The body scan is another profound mindfulness meditation technique that encourages a systematic exploration of the body to deepen self-awareness.

Begin with Breath Awareness

Start with a few minutes of mindful breathing to center yourself and settle into the practice.

Bring Attention to the Body

Direct your attention to different parts of your body, starting from the toes and moving up to the head. Notice any sensations, tension, or relaxation in each area.

Scanning with Care

As you scan, move your attention gently and systematically. If you encounter areas of tension or discomfort, allow your breath to soothe and release it.

A Comprehensive Journey

The body scan meditation is like taking a mental journey through your own body. It can reveal areas of tension or stress and provide an opportunity for healing and release.

Mindfulness meditation is a practice that can transform the way you relate to yourself and the world around you. It's about embracing the present moment, appreciating its richness, and living with greater awareness. As you continue to explore mindfulness, you'll develop a deeper connection with yourself and experience the bliss that arises from living in the here and now.

Chapter 10
What is Mindful Living?

In this chapter, we'll delve into the heart of mindful living, seeking to understand what it truly means and why it is so essential in our fast-paced world.

Defining Mindfulness

Mindfulness is often described as the practice of paying deliberate, non-judgmental attention to the present moment. It is the art of being fully engaged with your thoughts, feelings, bodily sensations, and the environment around you. Mindfulness invites you to experience each moment as it unfolds, without trying to change it or wishing it were different.

One of the fundamental aspects of mindfulness is awareness. It's about being aware of your thoughts, emotions, and bodily sensations without attaching judgment or labels to them. This non-judgmental awareness allows you to gain insight into your inner world and make wiser choices in response to life's challenges.

The Roots of Mindfulness

The practice of mindfulness has ancient roots that can be traced back to various spiritual and philosophical traditions. Perhaps one of the most well-known sources of mindfulness is Buddhism, where it is referred to as "sati" in Pali and "smṛti" in Sanskrit. The teachings of the Buddha emphasize the importance of mindfulness in attaining enlightenment and liberation from suffering.

However, mindfulness is not limited to Buddhism. It has deep connections with other spiritual traditions, such as Taoism, Hinduism, and the mystical aspects of Christianity and Islam. These traditions have their own variations of mindfulness practices, all geared toward developing self-awareness and achieving a deeper connection with the divine or the self.

In recent decades, mindfulness has transcended its religious and spiritual origins to become a secular practice embraced by people from all walks of life. It is no longer confined to the meditation cushion but has found its way into various fields, including psychology, medicine, education, and corporate wellness programs. The secular approach to mindfulness focuses on its mental and emotional benefits, making it accessible to individuals of diverse beliefs and backgrounds.

Why Mindfulness Matters

The practice of mindfulness has garnered a considerable amount of attention in the scientific and medical communities. Numerous studies have demonstrated its positive effects on mental and physical well-being. Here are some reasons why mindfulness matters:

Stress Reduction: Mindfulness helps individuals better manage and reduce stress. By learning to be present in the moment and observe their thoughts and emotions without judgment, people can reduce their reactivity to stressors.

Improved Emotional Regulation: Mindfulness equips individuals with tools to understand and regulate their emotions. This leads to greater emotional intelligence and resilience in the face of life's challenges.

Enhanced Focus and Concentration: Regular mindfulness practice can improve one's ability to focus and concentrate. This is particularly beneficial in our information-saturated world.

Better Relationships: Mindfulness fosters empathy and compassion. When you're more attuned to your own emotions and those of others, you can improve the quality of your relationships.

Greater Self-Awareness: Mindfulness encourages self-reflection and self-awareness. It helps you understand your patterns of thought and behavior, allowing for personal growth and change.

Physical Health Benefits: There is evidence to suggest that mindfulness can positively impact physical health. It has been linked to reduced blood pressure, improved immune function, and better sleep.

As we explore further in this book, you'll discover practical techniques and exercises that will enable you to incorporate mindfulness into your daily life. From mindful breathing to body scan meditations, you'll have a toolkit of practices to choose from as you embark on your journey toward mindful living.

Chapter 11

The Origins and Evolution of Meditation

Meditation, an ancient practice that has transcended time and culture, finds its roots in the deep annals of human history. From the contemplative practices of early civilizations to its present-day prominence, meditation has evolved, diversified, and seamlessly integrated into various cultures and religions worldwide.

Historical Roots in Ancient Civilizations

The origins of meditation can be traced back over 5,000 years to ancient civilizations such as India and China. In the Indian subcontinent, the earliest recorded meditation practices were documented in the Vedas, ancient sacred texts dating back to around 1500 BCE.

The teachings of Indian sages and ascetics, notably in the form of yogic practices, emphasized meditation to attain spiritual enlightenment and self-realization.

In China, Taoist and Confucian traditions also embraced meditative practices, focusing on harmony with nature and self-reflection.

Beyond Asia, meditation found its way into the ancient cultures of Egypt, where hieroglyphs depict meditation poses, and Greece, where philosophers like Pythagoras practiced deep contemplation.

Indigenous cultures in Africa, the Americas, and Australia also had their unique forms of meditative practices, often intertwined with rituals, ceremonies, and connecting with the natural world.

Development and Diversification Across Cultures and Religions

As human societies evolved and expanded, so did the practice of meditation.

Diverse cultures and religions adopted and adapted meditation to suit their beliefs and spiritual goals. In Buddhism, meditation became a principal component, with various techniques developed to achieve mindfulness and enlightenment.

Similarly, in Hinduism, meditation was a vital part of the yogic tradition, aimed at transcending the limitations of the mind and body.

In the Islamic tradition, Sufi mystics practiced meditation to attain a closer connection with the divine. Christian mystics in the medieval period engaged in contemplative prayer and meditation, seeking communion with God.

In Japan, Zen Buddhism emphasized meditation to experience direct, intuitive insight into reality.

Modern Adaptations and the Integration of Meditation in Contemporary Lifestyles

The 20th and 21st centuries witnessed a significant resurgence of interest in meditation, spurred by globalization, scientific exploration, and the quest for inner peace amid the fast-paced modern world. Meditation traveled from its traditional settings to the West, where it underwent various adaptations.

In contemporary times, meditation has become an integral part of many secular contexts.

It is widely used in healthcare settings to alleviate stress, manage chronic pain, and promote overall well-being. Meditation has found its way into educational institutions, the corporate world, and even prisons, where it is recognized for its potential in enhancing focus, creativity, and emotional regulation.

With the rise of technology, meditation has also found a home in the digital realm. Meditation apps, online courses, and virtual communities provide accessible platforms for individuals to learn and practice meditation techniques, making this ancient art form relevant and accessible to people from all levels of society.

In this ever-changing landscape, the essence of meditation as a path to inner peace and self-discovery continues to endure, reminding us of the timeless wisdom encapsulated in the quietude of contemplation.

Chapter 12

Establishing Your Mindfulness Practice

Creating the Foundation

Now that we have laid the conceptual groundwork for mindfulness meditation in Chapter 1, it's time to dive into the practicalities. Chapter 2 serves as your guide to initiate and establish a mindfulness practice, creating a solid foundation for the transformative journey ahead.

Setting the Scene: Creating Your Mindful Space

The first step in establishing your mindfulness practice is to designate a space conducive to inner reflection. This doesn't necessitate an elaborate meditation room; it can be as simple as a quiet corner in your home. What matters most is that it is a place where you feel comfortable and free from distractions. Consider adding elements that promote a sense of calm, such as a cushion, a soft blanket, or perhaps a small plant.

Choosing Your Posture: Finding Comfort and Presence

Mindfulness can be practiced in various physical postures, but finding one that is comfortable and sustainable is crucial. Whether sitting on a chair, cushion, or even lying down, the key is to maintain an upright and alert posture. This not only supports attentiveness but also helps cultivate a sense of presence in the moment.

Consistency is Key: Establishing a Routine

Mindfulness, like any skill, benefits from regular practice. Consider starting with short sessions, perhaps 5-10 minutes, and gradually extending the duration as you become more accustomed to the practice. Consistency is more important than duration—frequent, shorter sessions are often more effective than sporadic, lengthy ones.

Establishing a routine involves finding a time that suits your schedule. It could be in the morning, during a lunch break, or before bedtime. The goal is to integrate mindfulness into your daily life in a way that feels sustainable and enjoyable.

The Breath as Your Anchor: Initiating Breath Awareness

With your mindful space and posture established, turn your attention to the breath—an anchor that grounds you in the present moment. Begin by simply observing the natural rhythm of your breath. Notice the sensation of the breath entering and leaving your body. If your mind wanders, gently bring your focus back to the breath.

Breath awareness serves as a powerful tool not only during formal meditation but also in moments of stress throughout the day. Cultivating this awareness allows you to access a sense of calm whenever you need it.

Overcoming Common Challenges: Patience and Persistence

As you embark on your mindfulness journey, it's essential to approach the practice with patience and a gentle persistence. It's normal for the mind to wander, and moments of restlessness or frustration may arise. Instead of viewing these as obstacles, consider them part of the learning process. Gently guide your attention back to the present moment, and over time, you'll find that your ability to stay focused improves.

Tracking Progress: Journaling and Reflection

Consider keeping a mindfulness journal to track your progress and reflect on your experiences. Note any insights, changes in your mental state, or challenges you encounter. This practice not only enhances self-awareness but also provides a record of your mindfulness journey, showing the evolution of your practice over time.

Sharing the Journey: Building a Mindful Community

While mindfulness is often a personal practice, sharing your journey with others can provide valuable support and motivation. Whether joining a local meditation group, participating in online communities, or simply discussing your experiences with friends, building connections with fellow practitioners can enhance your mindfulness journey.

As Chapter 2 draws to a close, you've laid the foundation for your mindfulness practice. With a dedicated space, a consistent routine, and the breath as your guide, you're now ready to deepen your exploration of mindfulness meditation in the chapters that follow. Remember, the journey is as important as the destination, and each moment of mindful awareness is a step towards a more balanced and centred life.

Chapter 13

Embracing Mindfulness and Meditation

Understanding the Importance of Mindfulness and Meditation

In our fast-paced and demanding world, women in midlife often find themselves juggling multiple responsibilities and facing new challenges. It is during this transformative period that the importance of mindfulness and meditation becomes even more evident. These ancient practices offer profound benefits for our physical, emotional, and mental wellbeing, making them essential tools for women in midlife and beyond. Mindfulness is about being fully present in the moment, paying attention to our thoughts, feelings, and surroundings without judgment. By cultivating this awareness, we can develop a deeper understanding of ourselves and our experiences. For women in midlife, this can be a time of self-reflection and rediscovery, where mindfulness allows us to embrace the changes and challenges that come with ageing gracefully. Meditation, on the other hand, is a practice that involves focusing the mind and achieving a state of calmness and clarity. It allows us to quiet the noise of our thoughts and find inner peace. As women, we may be dealing with various physical and emotional changes. Meditation can help us navigate these transitions with grace, reducing stress, anxiety, and depression. It can also improve our ability to cope with pain and enhance our overall sense of wellbeing.

The benefits of mindfulness and meditation extend beyond our mental and emotional health. Research has shown that these practices can have a positive impact on our physical health as well. They can lower blood pressure, improve sleep quality, boost the immune system, and even slow down the ageing process. Taking care of our bodies becomes increasingly important, and mindfulness and meditation provide effective means to achieve holistic wellness.

By incorporating mindfulness and meditation into our daily lives, we can cultivate a deep sense of self-awareness, resilience, and inner peace. These practices can help us find balance, reduce stress, and enhance our overall wellbeing as we navigate this transformative stage of life.

"The Wisdom Within: Mindfulness and Meditation for Empowered Female Ageing" is a comprehensive guide that explores the specific needs and challenges faced by women in midlife and beyond. It provides practical techniques, exercises, and insights to help women establish a meaningful mindfulness and meditation practice. Whether you are new to these practices or have some experience, this book offers valuable tools to support your journey towards a healthier and more fulfilling life.

Embrace the wisdom within and discover the transformative power of mindfulness and meditation. It is never too late to begin this journey of self-discovery and self-care. Start today and unlock the full potential of your mind, body, and spirit.

Benefits of Mindfulness and Meditation for Women

As women enter midlife and beyond, they often find themselves at a crossroads of life. With the many roles they have played throughout the years – as caregivers, professionals, partners, and friends – it is not uncommon for women to feel a sense of overwhelm and uncertainty about what lies ahead. This is where the powers of mindfulness and meditation come into play, offering a multitude of benefits specifically tailored to the needs of mature women.

One of the key advantages of mindfulness and meditation for mature women is the ability to find inner peace and tranquility. These practices provide a space for self-reflection, helping women to reconnect with their true selves and gain a deeper understanding of their desires, needs, and aspirations. By cultivating a sense of mindfulness, women can navigate this transformative phase of life with clarity and grace.

Additionally, mindfulness and meditation have been proven to reduce stress and anxiety, which can be particularly prevalent during this stage of life. The hormonal changes brought on by menopause often lead to mood swings and emotional distress. Through mindfulness and meditation, women can learn to manage these fluctuations more effectively, promoting emotional well-being and overall mental health. Furthermore, as we age, we may face physical challenges that come with the natural process of getting older. Mindfulness and meditation

practices can help alleviate symptoms of chronic pain and improve overall physical well-being. By focusing on the present moment and developing a non- judgmental awareness of their bodies, women can cultivate a greater sense of acceptance and gratitude for their physical selves. In addition to the numerous individual benefits, mindfulness and meditation can also enhance social connections and relationships. As women transition into this next phase of life, they may find themselves seeking deeper connections with others. Mindfulness practices can improve empathy, compassion, and communication skills, enabling women to build stronger and more fulfilling relationships with their loved ones.
In conclusion, mindfulness and meditation offer a wide range of benefits specifically tailored to the needs of mature women. From finding inner peace and reducing stress to improving physical well- being and enhancing social connections,

these practices can empower women to embrace this transformative stage of life with grace and resilience. By incorporating mindfulness and meditation into their daily routines, women can unlock the wisdom within and live a more fulfilling and purposeful life.

Chapter 14

A Simplified Guide for Beginners

If you're stepping into the world of meditation as a newcomer, the prospect of starting a personal practice might seem a bit daunting. With countless meditation techniques available, ranging from beginner to advanced, simplicity becomes your greatest ally. For those taking their first steps, the key is to keep it simple. This chapter serves as a guide for beginners, outlining primary steps to initiate and sustain your meditation practice.

Keep an Open Mind:

Understand that meditation is a journey that unfolds with practice. Approach it with an open mind, allowing yourself the space to learn and grow.

Choose a Type of Meditation:

Pick one that is best for you. For the purpose of this book, our focus will be on guided meditation and scripts, particularly suitable for beginners.

Select a Time and Place:
Find a time and place that suits you best. While a morning meditation routine is recommended, choose a time that aligns with your schedule. Consistency is crucial.

Prepare for Relaxation:

Create a calming environment in which you won't be disturbed. Silence electronic devices and wear comfortable clothing. Treat this as a moment of self-care. If meditating midday or during work, consider using noise-canceling headphones or calming music.

Commit to Daily Practice:

The benefits of meditation accrue over time, so plan to meditate a little each day. One-and-done sessions are less effective compared to consistent, daily practice.

Set a Time Limit:

For beginners, aim for a session lasting five to ten minutes. A manageable duration that facilitates the development of your meditation practice.

Choose Your Posture:

Whether sitting or standing, the choice is yours. Close your eyes or lower your gaze for a more inward-focused experience.

Sense Your Body:

Make final adjustments to enhance your comfort, heightening your awareness of your body and its sensations.

Focus on Your Breath:

Direct your attention to your breath as a focal point. The act of mindful breathing helps anchor your wandering mind.

Acknowledge Distractions:

It's normal for your mind to wander. Notice distractions and gently bring your focus back to your breath, using it as a tool for re-centering.

Reflect on Your Session:
After completing your meditation, take a moment to notice how you feel. Allow any emotions to surface without judgment. Meditation is a journey, so be kind to yourself. Consider jotting down your reflections to track your progress over time in a journal.

Embarking on the "how to meditate" journey may seem easier said than done, and occasional lapses are natural. If you miss a day or two, simply resume your practice as soon as possible. In the upcoming chapters, I will expand upon the specific benefits associated with shorter meditation sessions and explore how guided meditation scripts can assist.

Chapter 15

Getting Started with Mindfulness Meditation

If you're new to mindfulness meditation, it can be challenging to know where to begin. However, with practice and learning, you can quickly become comfortable with the basics.

Here are some tips on how to meditate for beginners:

Find a Quiet Spot

Choose a quiet spot where you won't be disturbed for the duration of your meditation. This could be a room in your house or a peaceful spot in nature.

Get Comfortable

Sit comfortably in a chair or on the floor, with your back straight but not rigid. You can also lie down if you prefer, but be aware that you may fall asleep.

Focus on Your Breath

Breathe in deeply through your nose for four seconds. Hold your breath for seven seconds, and then exhale loudly through your mouth for eight seconds. Repeat this process several times until you feel relaxed.

Bring Mindfulness into Meditation

It can be helpful to bring mindfulness into your meditation. One way to do this is to consciously be aware of your senses. Once you're comfortable, close your eyes and then focus on each of your other senses. What can you hear? What can you smell? What can you feel?

Practice Regularly

Like any skill, mindfulness meditation takes practice. Start with just a few minutes a day and gradually increase the time as you become more comfortable. Try to practice at the same time each day to make it a habit.

By following these tips, you'll be on your way to mastering mindfulness meditation and enjoying its many benefits.

Chapter 16

Preparing for Meditation

Before you begin meditating, it's important to set yourself up for success. Here are some tips to help you prepare for your meditation practice:

Find a comfortable seat

Choose a comfortable seat that allows you to sit with a straight spine and relaxed body. You can sit on a cushion, bench, or chair, as long as it supports your legs and bottom. Make sure your feet are flat on the ground and your hands are resting comfortably on your lap.

Focus on your breath

Take a few deep breaths to help you relax and focus your mind. Pay attention to your breath as it enters and leaves your body. You can count your breaths or simply observe the sensation of your breath moving in and out of your body.

Relax your body

Scan your body for any tension and consciously release it. Start at the top of your head and work your way down to your toes. You can also do a few gentle stretches to help release any tension in your body.

Set an intention

Before you begin your meditation practice, set an intention for what you hope to achieve. This can be as simple as wanting to feel more relaxed or focused, or as specific as wanting to cultivate more compassion or gratitude.

Be patient and kind to yourself

Remember that meditation is a practice, and it takes time and patience to develop. Be kind to yourself and don't judge yourself if your mind wanders or you find it difficult to focus. Simply acknowledge the thought or distraction and gently bring your focus back to your breath.

By following these simple steps, you can create a comfortable and supportive environment for your meditation practice. Remember to be patient and kind to yourself, and don't be discouraged if it takes time to develop your practice. With regular practice, you will begin to experience the many benefits of mindfulness meditation.

Chapter 17

Body Scan Meditation

Body scan meditation is a mindfulness exercise that involves focusing your attention on different parts of your body, from the top of your head to the tips of your toes. The purpose of this exercise is to help you become more aware of your body and any sensations you may be feeling. To do a body scan meditation, find a quiet place where you can lie down comfortably. Close your eyes and bring your attention to your breath. Then, slowly scan your body from head to toe, noticing any sensations you may be feeling. If you notice any tension or discomfort, try to relax those areas by taking a deep breath and releasing the tension as you exhale.

2. Awareness of Breath Meditation

Awareness of breath meditation is another basic mindfulness technique that involves focusing your attention on your breath. The purpose of this exercise is to help you become more aware of your breath and any thoughts or distractions that may arise. To do this exercise, find a quiet place where you can sit comfortably. Close your eyes and bring your attention to your breath. Notice the sensation of the air moving in and out of your nostrils. If your mind wanders, gently bring your attention back to your breath.

Mindful Walking

Mindful walking is a simple mindfulness exercise that involves walking slowly and deliberately, paying attention to your body and surroundings. To do this exercise, find a quiet place where you can walk without any distractions. Start by taking a few deep breaths and bringing your attention to your body. Then, begin walking slowly and deliberately, noticing the sensation of your feet touching the ground and the movement of your body. If your mind wanders, gently bring your attention back to your body and surroundings.

Mindful Eating

Mindful eating is a mindfulness exercise that involves paying attention to the taste, texture, and sensation of each bite of food you eat. To do this exercise, choose a small piece of food, such as a raisin or a small piece of chocolate. Take a few deep breaths and bring your attention to the food. Then, slowly and deliberately take a bite, noticing the taste, texture, and sensation of the food in your mouth. Chew slowly and mindfully, paying attention to the sensation of the food as you swallow.

5. Mindful Breathing

Mindful breathing is a simple mindfulness exercise that involves focusing your attention on your breath. To do this exercise, find a quiet place where you can sit comfortably. Close your eyes and bring your attention to your breath. Notice the sensation of the air moving in and out of your nostrils. If your mind wanders, gently bring your attention back to your breath.

These basic mindfulness meditation techniques can help you develop your awareness, attention, and focus. With regular practice, you can learn to apply these techniques to your daily life, helping you to become more mindful and present in each moment.

www.ingramcontent.com/pod-product-compliance
Lightning Source LLC
LaVergne TN
LVHW010552070526
838199LV00063BA/4952